A Walk *of* *Many* Paths

D.M. FERGUSON

STRATTON
—PRESS—

Publishing Life

Stratton Press Publishing
831 N Tatnall Street Suite M #188,
Wilmington, DE 19801
www.stratton-press.com
1-888-323-7009

Because of the dynamic nature of the Internet, any web addresses or
links contained in this book may have changed since publication and
may no longer be valid. The views expressed in the work are solely those
of the author and do not necessarily reflect the views of the publisher,
and the publisher hereby disclaims any responsibility for them.

ISBN (Paperback): 978-1-64895-549-5
ISBN (Ebook): 978-1-64895-550-1

Printed in the United States of America

For those who have experienced the horrors of the reality of the foster care system and to those who had to learn to survive completely on their own.

I learned that courage was not the absence of fear, but the triumph over it. The brave man is not he who does not feel afraid, but he who conquers that fear.

—Nelson Mandela

CONTENTS

Part Two: Other Memories of the Crows

Part One:

Growing Up a Crow

Crows and Ravens

Bad luck for us black birds is our shadow,
As we are branded with many unsavoury personas, like trickster
Or ill-omened outcast. Castaways.

No matter how broken our speech sounds,
the mere utterances of our pained cawing spark repulsion.

How many chances are they going to take with our lives?
That is the caretakers, whose job it is to feed us, house us,
And most importantly, care for us.

I'm cursed. We are cursed.
Within these rust-eaten iron cages,
Our only odds are fight or flight.

But my wings are clipped, so it's pointless.
Still, I will fight with claw and beak.
I am dubbed the freedom fighter.

Even if I remain locked in this iron cell.

Crevasses split inside my cerebral domain.
My bony mandibles click and chatter.
My once gentle heart throbs in rage,
When hot tears flow from my deep-black pupils.

All the while, hunger consumes all my thoughts.

So peck, claw, snap at the locks.
While screeching the dialect, everyone has forgotten.
This is the dialect of kindness and kind words.
To them, we are voiceless.
Oh, yes, the caretakers toss in grain,
And splash in water from their silver jugs.

But, contrary to their name, they are careless!

This occurred to me, the Crow, till one hand unlocked the door.
I pecked—blood trickled down her hand.
I clawed—struggling to breathe in sweet fresh air.
I hopped—I hopped from that suffocating cage.
Willingly, I followed the old woman in the billowing
white cloak…

Never to return to the Caretaker's household.

Utopian Family Matters

Firstborn birth is celebrated.

Henceforth a father's flame is ignited,
while mother's strings are deeply implanted.

Father's smoke leeches the air from his own
child, for he is born with no breath.

Thrown into the breathing box for a time.
He was born to survive.

After a fight with his insanity,
The social service summoned their authority
To take the child—stolen in the mental one's eyes,
Though witnesses would say otherwise.

Portraying the flawless family mirror,
within which the SS saw through the tiny dysfunctional crack.

Five years have passed with their second chance.
Mother won the right to raise.

Returning to the original state, being praised.
Within this victory—something festered, unawares.

Soon another event will bring its hammer down,
causing the irreparable blight on this utopian family.

This union will deteriorate into dust.

Fragmenting all null and void.
Filled with the stripes of flame, the ache
of delirium, of hollow security and belonging.

His world, struck with thunder.
Emerged out of this lone survivor.

And the hellish demons will be unleashed.

D.M. FERGUSON

Beast of the Mind

It lies slumbering, deep in the crevasses.
Here in the perfect four of a kind family.
His flames engorge wildly within,
And so, unshaven, unclean, unruly, so strange.
This is a mind of many—not one.

The cracks sink deeper—ever expanding its grip.
All his sense of reasoning—flushed out
And so, the derangement of the beast is set loose.
It will haunt the futures of all who witness
The onset of the creature that only consumes.

All secure parental barriers shatter—utterly
Knowing it will never be capable, to hold itself back
From delving into the great seven sins.

Like the devil's fury, that burns all.
The full effect
would not be fully understood…

Till years later.

Child's Purity

Born, we are clean slates.

We are all put in a heavenly state.
Our first sages introduce selfish insanity,
Not assisted by their polluted environments,
Despite them pouring holy water all over it.

Our unfathomable reality,
All come to believe the real causality.

Although we are given hypnotic drugs,
That impose someone else's beliefs.

We are lost to the influence of the system.

Torn away from all we know.

For we are forcibly chained to the system
set to purify the offspring of broken families,
of those who droned religiously about our protection.
Does that make us into tradable goods?

Think about the rippling effects on us—
On our most impressable and malleable minds—
It all destroys our sense of feeling.
which will leave us all reeling.

Unless we learn to stow our feelings and survive.

Reality of the Ward

I'm finding life to be a grim ordeal.
I dream—determined to find my fate.
I cannot fathom, whether this is all real.

For these true events are completely surreal.
I fantasize in the kinder dream state.
I'm finding life to be a grim ordeal.

Whilst in these hardships, I find it hard to feel.
In this bombardment of tricks and lies, I wait
and I cannot fathom whether this is all real.

Life presents greater fear, but how won't I keel?
My shaky strength must endure and await as still,
I'm finding life to be a grim ordeal.

I must, by god, I must not squeal,
despite their actions infecting me with hate
while I cannot fathom whether this is all real.

I'm keeping my shields high in this spiel.
I'm sure all of you can understand and relate.
I'm finding life to be a grim ordeal
I cannot fathom whether this is all real.

House of the Beast
Part I

For the first time, I enter the house of smoke and ash,
  Where the air all around is a poisonous fume.
 For every breath, there taken, leaves me wheezing
 And on every counter, there stood, several towers
All splotched with unidentifiable solids and sauces.

  I see the dirt ingrained in the carpet floors.
 Dead insects clogged, all of them dry and hollow
    Inside the dust-covered window sills.
  Deep in the living room den, inside the ashtray
   In the centre of the stained coffee table,
Were the ugly sight of the previously smoked smokes.

 And there it was, lying on his throne of indolence.
Mummy, now tending to his every need—rolling his cigs,
 Providing him with his addictions—supplying him,
  Ensuring the advancement of this beastly beast,
Wearing nothing more than the stained unclean boxers.

 Being set down on the ground—I stare trembling
   Intimidation settles into my mindset
 For the hairy beast breathed heavy cigarette smoke
  Blowing a plume in the blankness of my face.
   Oh god, how am I now safe here?

   I see myself locked in with it.
 I see myself wanting to leave—to escape this den.
  A mix of fear and rage leaks into me,
  Spreading across my world like wildfire.
  Retroactively, I was placed in this hell!

Awakening of the Beast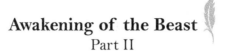
Part II

I

Awakening from a deep slumber, I came to realize,
The unusual calmness of the great beast's foreboding home;
I notice the steadiness of steady breath—
Soundless from the whiner's bedchamber.
I sigh, for this other boy next door is for once silent.
Till this time, the other beasts have yet to become violent.

Whatever are the symptoms, but the festering
Mental influence within this family? Today all will crack!
I throw my covers over with the urge to pee,
My lungs gasp, as I pass the wafts of urine.
That bedchamber where the other boy slept—is he conscious?
Or obliviously nose-blind? The urine scent is toxic.

A deep breath of revitalization!
An escape into the room of relief, the main bathroom,
Which wasn't entirely clean with the pubic hair bundles!
A urine stain is encrusted at the toilet base—
The bundles rolling across, the stained surface,
All collectively creating a mild disturbance.

My timid soul, like some swelled cancerous cell,
Keeps me silenced in a still grave. How quiet is quiet?
The sleeping beast, I gaze into its chamber.
This creature snores loudly, and all unshaven, all unclean,
And the beast is a beast, free to create a murderous scene.

II

Once down the winding stairs, whilst thinking, wearily
and cautiously,
Over many a thought of the rage of the beast,
Whilst the scent of nicotine entered my nostrils, I peer over,
As if I am cleverly spying, spying into the lion's den.
"No one's here," I whispered, "lying in the lion's den—
Now I can go, and crossover."

Sigh, I recall the bareness and the filthiness,
And the overall messiness itself embedded into my memory.
Fervently I searched the cupboards—meekly seeking a
clean glass
Where upon the high shelves I discovered—discovered a
clean cup—
For I climbed and clamored upon the contaminated counter for
this cup—
Examining its spotlessness and looking it over.

And the sullen expression of my sad fancy swept over me
Leaking in me—imbuing me with a fowl stench;
As I gazed inside the bright and empty fridge, I stood gaping,
"Nothing much is here, and what is has expired—
I wondered, was it the cheese? The yogurt? Yes, the milk
hadn't expired—
It wasn't much, but I poured the remaining bit over."

Currently my senses were null, perceiving my awareness dull,
"Dad?" I muttered. "Mum, whoever is coming down, I wonder,
But truly I was so nervous, and so quickly I jumped breathless,
And I look toward the stairwell, the stairwell where I shudder,
Whether my mother or father came down"—cause at the sight
of either I shudder—
Knowing the pain, they both deliver.

Deep in the clutches of half-sleep, long awoke to crave and
reap,
Shortly to consume a hot pot of sugar-filled coffee before
the games.
"Naturally," I muttered, "naturally this cannot be just a
normal day,"
Yet silence remained almost deafening, and the calmness no
less threatening;
This I felt while I stare up at the beast as it passed by—
Playing absently, trying not to quiver.

III

Suddenly standing there in front, it seemed he was on a
playful hunt,
Where something caught my wondering eye, so it seemed its
eyes widened.
"Surely," I uttered, "surely you shan't be just playing.
So kindly let me down, and do not turn my being
upside down—
Gently place me on the ground and let me play on my own—
This I wish, so please reconsider."

It was then I was flipped, with little to no emotion
And within the greasy and hair-covered face, smiled with
dark pleasure;
Not the least forgiving given he, had not an ounce of sanity,

But when I came to realize the futility, the tears streamed—
Letting me drop from high above, he smiled as my
tears streamed—
He glared, and smiled with the pain delivered.

Then this unstable beast, feeding upon my cries in
more violence,
By the unhinged and cracked mind of the beast, he struck me.
"What had I done? Why oh why do I deserve this pain," I cried.
Enraged he continued with every bruising thunderous stroke—
"Tell me what I've done? I didn't do anything to need these
bruising strokes,"
I spoke attempting to negotiate.

Fleeing, scampering up the stairs, I escaped into my mother's
bed chamber,
So shortly I heard more thuds ripping, ripping through the
whole home.
Bursting through, my mother with child tight in arm, they
rushed in;
Slamming the door, locking it tight, we all sat holding each
other on the bed—
What this grave, fowl, near demonic, unfeeling and fear-
inducing beast
Meant that this will never be truly over.

IV

This I pondered whilst my security cracked, but in no
way unbacked
To the extinguishing flames of fatherhood, and the severing of
the strings of motherhood.
Independence, now greatly sought, I must believe it was not
for naught;
For all sense of love and happiness leak through my pores—
With wave unto wave of inequitable silence, when the front
door was slammed.

And so, my foundation shattered and keeled over.

"Mother," I asked, "will you call the cops?" Disturbing, still it
was, if possessed or premediated,
Whether his temper blew, or whether he used his temper to
excuse desire to strike,
Desperate to rid me unwanted—taking extremes to leave
me daunted
By this beast through unwarranted horror—please say you'll
make the call—
Is there—is there any reason not to? Please say—please say
you'll make the call—
Hesitating, taking a breath, she agreed and dialed.

And so, the seeds of depression planted, with the feeling of
rage branded,
I must remain tepid and courageous, just to survive and endure,
And despite it fleeing before me, I must not falter into a
drunken boor
And my heart shall see through the encroaching darkness and
survive pure,
Knowing never to let self-pity spill over,
poison me, and take over.

The World Outside to the Gentle Ward

I

Observe

the ward who awaits freedom,
heart skipping as those worn records,
with the imminence of the savior's arrival

into a chaotic and polluted home front,
waiting to experience the world outside.

She is coming,

Her car hums patiently in park.
She walks up and knocks,
This day is no ordinary day,
as the ward jumped all excited and grateful,
as he is about to greet the world outside.

He's on a probationary trip to the city,
Greater than the mostly rural town he is from!
Learning to breathe again, he takes in fresh air
Long expulsed from the cesspool prisonlike home,
So, this is what it's like to be in the world outside.

The little ward arrives at the kid's festival,
that swarms of them flood the walkways.
White tents standing tall
With excitement filling all the kiddies
Waiting as is the ward to enjoy the world outside.

Aromas caress and fondle with the ward's nose.
These mouth-watering scents have yet to reach him.
As prior, the only smells were smoke and filth
Damn near drooling, he pronounces his desire to try,
And taste these cuisines of the world outside.

II

Many activities—everywhere,
So much to do, yet time is short
For the ward chooses his time delicately
Knowing the preset limitations,
Not yet realizing this clear confusion about the world outside.

One does catch his wandering eye,
Noticing the cues of children at this certain tent,
Each of them returning with a different face;
Of a different colour and with various weird patterns
Thinking about the strangeness of the world outside.

Deeply desiring to join in,
The lucky ward jumped in
And asked for the painters to paint
His face a different colour,
A colour reflecting the true-blue feeling from the world outside.

Anxiety swept over the ward's brain,
For fear of the rage of the warden,
As she stresses on who has the keys
And who has given such limited time,
For the ward was made to fear the world outside.

Conflicted between choosing
To stay and enjoy or leave and lack
The fulfilling need for social need
And become arrested by the stern grip
Projected by the charade of the world outside.
So, the ward is cautious
Of the enjoyment of the world outside
And thus, desires to leave.

Waltzing through the Yearly Solstice

Their maple leaves gliding to their funerals.

Their trees unveiling their true colours.

I have once attempted to change my undeserved fate.

Like whistling gusts that dance with the fallen,

Like rakes waltzing with their various partners.

I have whirled around from place to place.
I've treated you distantly.
I hope you would forgive me.
If I have hurt you.

I hope you won't pity me, as it wasn't on purpose.

The Blind Choices of the Ward

These choices! Oh, these blind choices!
Spinning around me, this carousel of choices!
How confusing the lord's layout, there shown?
With my life being withheld from the secure throne.
From the safe and happy throne—
From the insular, comforting, rewarding throne,
Of my life, which is a carousel of choices, blind choices,
straight choices—
Of blind choices!

These choices! Oh, these heavy choices!
Flying at me, this chain of heavy choices!
How in contempt with the sight of letdown
With the system being upheld in their playground.
In their precarious and random playground—
In their cold, unforgiving, uncaring playground,
Of my life, which is a movie reel of choices, heavy choices,
doubtful choices—
Of heavy choices!

These choices! Oh, these guilty choices!
Piercing my being, this bombardment of choices!
How angering this turn of unfortunate events
Due to the exchange of fiery intent.
Of this misunderstood and questionable intent—
Of this indiscernible, uncertain, worrisome intent,
With my life, which is becoming a laundry list of choices,
Guilty choices, impossible choices—
Of guilty choices!

Desires of the Depraved

We've returned! We've returned!
Is there much we have learned?
From the beast now caged, bound, and sedated,
Since he had raged upon me, whom now I indefinitely hated.

Presently distractions keep me at bay;
Those screens flash, oh how they helped this day?
Once secure, broken, caught—now hoped in vain
Now our beings slump down in pain.

Sitting there in front of the glass screen,
two towers in a billowing black smoke scene,
thinking about things with growing strain,
about this darn situation and this darn life chain.

And so, mother walks up and flips it off
These episodes may continue and set me off,
While the world too is now devoid of security
My own desires remain to desire to fill the void.

Daunting Haven on the Hill

In the lushest of rolling hills
By grey squirrels populated,
Maybe once a cheery and homely haven—
Respected haven—stares me down.
In the sound of the departing bus —
A coldness swept over us!
Never has gooseflesh spread so quick
Over my entire being—the presence daunting!

Doors pitch black, heavy iron, foreboding
To its visitors, opened with an ear-piercing whine,
(This foyer—much like others—gave the same notion
Of uncomfortable silence).

And every white coat which marched,
Between the connecting corridors
Followed the wandering crazies down those halls,
Meanwhile scorned screams echoed through the walls.

A curmudgeon in that indignant haven,
By whom greeted us three wishful lambs, saw
Listless hope swimming in their pupils,
While mother makes her inquiry of her precious beast,
When the reply said, "Sixth floor, room 666."
(The red demon itself, inside its den.)
In a manner of near force rightfully so,
Brother and I were dragged to the old elevator.

And with all the exhausted gears singing
Was the opening of the rust-eaten doors,
Through which we will dawn upon its new cage,
Some loony sits in a corner, "Why are you here? Why?
Why? Why?"
Ever hollering and trembling
It shakes, it shakes uncontrollably.
Each utterance of each jittery question
Shook me—shook me to my core.
But demonic things, cloaked in a shadow of fear
Consumed the mind's sense of courage.
(Must we open it? The hell now surely trapped beyond.
Must we visit him, the beast which struck.)
And mother grasped the dullen brass knob
That whined and retorted,
Is but another reminder of why
"I would leave it rotting!"

The Walk of Many Paths

In the shaded woods, I wandered down
my eyes skewered
by conflicting beliefs.
My angry visage
kissed by the breeze.
There was a calming presence beneath the oaks,
the underbrush.

Advisors preach.
Fragile emotions are beings
that shattered me.

How can one find trust
in the ten thousand preachers in child care
with their unspoken intentions revealing themselves?

These darkened woods.
These paths.
The one must choose.
Makes me rigid
in a world
where all claim to be better.

And so, I read, but little into the thoughts of others

till I was given the one thing that needs to universally
be given...

and that's kindness.

Pimp Up Your Geek Day

The loneliest day—the loneliest hour,
Waning and fading confidence aching evermore,
belonging and security.

I felt has left me—ever ignored.

Friends? I claimed? Yes! No! Such is confused;

The tease of new friends has been,
But a day unknown to those not connected to Facebook.

Belonging. What do I know of such things?
New clothes: large hoodie, loose jeans, minus a golden chain.

They demand me to wear these things. I had shades too,
Even my hip sway was important.

The loneliest day—the loneliest hour
Eyes slowly opened— they'd never seen so clearly
The brightest of child welfare.
I did feel the fakeness among these "friends."

But then it was asked of me: to find a girl.

One who stands by my side, anytime I was seen outside.
Guiding me like a depraved puppy dog.
They have me a leash. I held the girl's hip.

For we both came under realization
Of the purpose of this sudden interest—understood
Reality and decided to divert.

I whispered in her ear, "Let's do our own thing."
We left them. Ignored them. We became true friends.

D.M. FERGUSON

The March of the Lone Wolf

No longer, the lone wolf aches,
He trots midstride. Breathes heavily;
Wishing upon the sedation of the past.
Inhibition of physical pain is gone.

Nor the passage of time has healed the many wounds.
Scar to scar, its effect permanent.
Every lashing sting of turbulent circumstance.
Hardened at the core of desperate survival.

Blowing winds pushing over through the firs.
Snow ankle-deep. His paws carrying him onward.
The lone wolf, gentle yet fierce.
In his silence. In his experience.

The pack that slashed him—
The others that shunned him—
Not dwell with its poison,
Lone wolf is to find his prey…

Dream Home on the Other Side

By my home bizarre and filthy,
Wrought by the ghosts of mental illness only,
Where for years and years and days and days,
I was chained to the origins of my past.
People walked through, seeing right through us
From the mindset of dismissible disgust—
From a state void of kindness, forgotten,
Out of mind—out of heart.

Sightless gazers and heartless workers,
And common senses, and regulations and rules,
Only one had enough sense to show me
And thus, alleviated the sting of the warden
Making kindness the one true nurturer
From the mindset of an old-fashioned doc
From a time when people were kinder, selfless
Making a dream home—making a dream family…
Introducing onto me the taste of probation.

The Beast's Heartfelt Warning

He didn't want the kid,
where he might bring him harm.

He warned them;
To listen, but present
And convince the uncaring minds,
But the peaceful hapless plea,
Wasn't going to reach the ear drums.

This is the price of ignorance.
The result of dismissing
the beast's warning…

And reality now comes knocking,
Like a wandering priest,
A shining sun projecting delirious delight.
Presently, this dark stain of ignorance grows,
And the bitter taste is only now coming through…
Anger stirs,
And the pot is full of kerfuffle.

An Old Log Cabin's Holiday

None more deserving of a holiday,
Moving from home to home, whereby inducing
Much stress needing much relief
Was cozy inside—inside this little cabin;

As seen in those showcases, the luxuries are spectacular,
Just like in those YouTube penthouse tours,
How the coziness of my room of dreams,
Compared to my own room in the less than regular home...
And so, I was given a taste of life beyond my current life.

The scenic scene, of the serenity here,
The expressive setting sun drifted further down:
And our beloved pooch wiggles her body happily,
Her stubby tail wagging rapidly.

This winter's chill grasps and settles,
Into the arches of our spines,
And the flocks of the withered, there drive
Away from all the kerfuffle there laid behind.

The Day the House Shook

I was young and she was wise,
In the old stucco rancher at the end;
But my imagination ran in my wild mind—
I thought I could hear;
With what wasn't there, that was my foolishness
Foreshadowing her and I.

And due to this on this day in spring,
In the old stucco rancher at the end,
She intended to prove they hadn't keeled over: the mice
So, I said repeatedly, "I heard them drop dead, I said!"
Last week, we found droppings,
And so, white powder was thrown all over in the attic:
In the night, I supposedly heard them
Drop dead in the old stucco rancher at the end.

The old wooden ladder, not half so well put together,
Was dragged out and stuck under the attic door—
Yes! This was the cause (as to the event that follows,
in the old stucco rancher at the end)
That the ladder creaked, wobbled, and cracked,
Knocking and causing the deterioration of the kind old doc.

It was yet another regular overcast day in spring,
In the old stucco rancher at the end,
That the doc there lived whom you may recall
As the hand that unlocked the cage;
And this doc she stood for no other reason,
Than to be kind and to be given kindness in return.

II

For she stepped on to the old wooden ladder
In the old rancher at the end;
And I who was about to hand her the marble lamp
In the old rancher at the end;
And I, who watched her mind black out
Everything shut down, she tipped over backward
And hemorrhaged when she struck her head,
And this fall shook the home at the end.
Thus, 911 is dialed, and the ambulances wail.

But still I went on up and shifted open the attic door
Of those areas whereby covered by shadows—
Of many imagined carcasses of dead mice—
And neither I who was already up there
Nor was the doc down at the base
Could have been aware of the next event
In the old stucco rancher at the end.

Within the Flames the Phoenix Rises

I, the ward, burned worn by tears to laughter,
From the many years, of clouds and smoke,
Hid my bright, kind, and gentle exterior away.
I, the ward, exhausted of feeling,
Feelings felt at once is too all they want!

I, the ward, burst into flames.
That we all have turned to crumpling ash,
Disheveled, hollowed wards turn,
Gaunt, desolate, and dark,
Falling, with their torn sensations.
Incented by plumes of disturbed dust.

I, the ward, desiring to survive.
Out from this here mess that I knew
On this rocky path, not so fair, is it?
Sighed for flames not so hot,
Field poppies scarlet and bright,
Growing out of the ashes, shaking them off.

I, the ward, too worn
Of the hopes and futures ahead!
Where the disheveled, hollowed wards turn,
Gaunt, desolate, and dark
Out of this pit and out of these ashes,
Rise as the risen phoenix in which I flew out...
And eventually I left it all behind
As best I, the ward, could.

Falling Leaves from the Parental Trees

The leaves are hanging on frailly onto their trees; curling
and changing,
Becoming emotional, emoting, brilliant colours we share:
Livening the day for others as for ours;
Yet wilting away we deceive them all, even ourselves!
About to dance us astray, the rakes come and hither;

Blown billows howled through pulling the leaves,
our futures fly into obscurity,
It affects us greatly—we'd sooner be
Home nuzzled against our parental framework;
So, may we stay, hanging onto this secure branch,
Have faith that would allow us to grow independently;
Have heart to not tear us from our only know security;
Listen to the rustling cries of fallen leaves.

They flit, float slowly down
Facing current realities, yet realizing their survivability rate,
challenging me and dancing to the beat of the last hour has
the power.

As one never knows when the figure of fate comes knocking!
The fate of leaves gambles, and cause them to crack,
Some may break. Crunch underneath
the foot falls of the oblivious passersby.

The Strange, the Change, the Acceptance

Accept all that happened—scars branded on flesh
Cranium battled, rugged, and hardened
by choices led by darker paths! Run! Be ruined!
Hurl against an electrified wall
Numbing out life once compared to soldiers, in wartime.

Each unfortunate case. Unveiling truth about the system.

Prompts. Old emotional campaigns reigning.
The unbelievable state of oppressive age.

Failing results—foster care would be helpful?
Aiding in troubled family matters, in such were needed.

Changes in strange matters.

Oh! This is the matter that amplifies the feeling.
Creating the doubts and despair of our hearts.

There is a but to this, that is to be believed,
Believing just one chapter.

And is all that you should know.

These dark chapters do end—

Only you can do so and let it go. Set yourself free.
With opportunities set in the future.

If only you choose to find the opportunity.
If only you choose to allow yourself to be helped…
Whatever clicks with you…
That's what I had to do.

D.M. FERGUSON

Paddling Out from Campbell River

Arrived in this city.
Ocean breeze blew blissfully.
Thick scent of decaying fish,
Thick with excitement within myself.

We all unload everything—we all check for everything,
Meticulously preparing for a trip across the sea.

We are ready.
Our floating vessels are set, ready to go steady.
Each kayak filled with the weight of our survival.
Each counselor planning our time of arrival.
At our first beach stop, have lunch.
Each of us dragging our kayaks to the lapping shores.

Sun ray's reflection, sparkles ripple
Across the intertwining currents between the Gulf Islands.

Paddling further out we reach open waters.
As we get tired, we rest upon a gulf island.
Onto the next one—till the wind picks up
As the waves slapping our plastic hulls.

The wind picked up wickedly.
We were pushed back.

We were forced to wait, till we decided,
to go ashore. Ask this family, if we could stay
and camp out on their lawn, till the storm passed.
since it would have been impossible to paddle through…
the gale force winds.

On we waited
Till the howling winds died.
Then we carried on.

Premonitions of the House of Blue

Dreamt of a house of blue.
Foreseen,
my time would end here in this safety dome.

Ah! Even as their health wanes
I understand the imperative reason
To depart and hand over the reins
Of the chariot ran by the demons.

This is one bad situation—this is one bad situation,
And, while they whisper behind closed doors,
They shove my being without cessation
Blissfully ignoring as they have for years.

What though lies beyond that door painted red,
That gold-knobbed door leading into the blue home—
What daunts me as I am here led
Into the new home under another cracked dome?

Now sitting, heart now racing in this first meeting,
Everyone gathered included the first ones—
Clearly, something wasn't right, something is heating
Inside the minds and hearts of these new ones.

What was I just tossed into?

Transitions in the House of Blue

Oh! All these choices made were completely misguided!
My tortured soul not fathoming, this life provided
Having been steeped inside a sweet cup of brandy.
Yes, it all went down easily as sugar-covered candy,
Till the throat was burning angrily, feeling groggily through

The variety of sweet bribes thereby they threw them over me
To cover up the cracks that grow evermore deeper
Cause it was increasingly apparent of how meager
Their financial stores were—that bi master of coin
Flipping—as the bipolar mummy trusted with coin
Thus, making for instability – should it have been given to her?

Whispers. Beware! In my ear once more.

My trust in them was fluttering as before,
As with the same family I was bred into before.

Prophet I call myself, thus seeing that dream unfold
Before my eyes evermore as this blue house turns
Blue internally, and things begin to sour.
Have I been placed in another devil's den?

The Perfect Masks of the House of Blue

Gaze upon this family fantasy!
Whereby, to the outsiders appeared,
Immaculately clean and tidy and well sorted—
You see no one could see the blemishes
In that an impeccable wondrous illusion;
Yet once you met and lived with them

For a night, or several more,
In this house of blue, full of perfect masks,
What is it they believe themselves to be?
All that seems to be all too perfect

Is, but the reason I never felt too comfortable.

I stand vacant with my expression
Whilst watching the new mother unravel,
And because I was myself an outsider.

A suitable target for her financial misgivings—

There were so many! Thinking me a thief, a taker
From the cupboard, also thinking me an abuser
Of animals: her cat was limping!

O Christ! She could not think me better
I who was no stealer—I who loved animals
In some ways, better than humans.

O Christ, why hadn't they been properly checked?
Clearly, she needed me though,
Only, however, it was more for the money,
And, seeing these cracks open, letting their true colours
Shine through…
And, finally, my shadow of bad luck still follows me.

Farmer's Market Waltz

I arrive all overcast in the city square.
Alone I waited on the bench—and on the bench
I opened my book reading till the trailer arrives.
Passing the time till the magic unit unveils itself,
Bringing forth the supplies needed for the waltz.

And when they arrive in the city square,
The show master whips out his blueprints
For this market community. For this pop-up show.
Preparing us—preparing us for the storm of busybodies
Yet to arrive and take part in the market waltz.

A key inside the padded lock is turned,
But before opening it, I hesitate,
Rubbing my eyes, yawning, lacking sleep,
From the previous night at the blue home.
Refocusing myself, I swung open the door for the waltz.

Time flies. Time whizzes away as we set up
Today's farmers' market waltz
With every tent of every colour,
Just as cars arrive. One after the other.
All which desire to sell in this here pop-up market.

Hours passed. Temperatures rose. Participants wandered
Through the lane of tents: All seeking refreshments.
I tended to the information giving in the centre
Handing pamphlets to passersby. Sweat was saturating.
Energies were draining in this farmers' market waltz.

Someone collapsed. People rushed over.
I heard someone say, "An ambulance was called."
The heat was record-breaking. I felt lightheaded myself.
We all waited. And waited. And waited.
No sirens. No medical personnel came to join the market waltz.

Half the hour passed, and finally help came.
In a timely fashion, the collapsed person was taken
And we thought, *We were so unprepared.*
Come closing time, we dismantled everything,
And went home to recover from today's market waltz.

Negligence: Chief of Social Service

Spoken with forked words
This creation fails,
Despite their kindest intentions
To project the perfect family unit
Generated by the chief of social service.

At the same time
With the same words
They tend to brush over
And powder the faces full of flaws
Utterly overlooked by the chief of social service.

Moving each of us around
Each case shuffled—abound
To make their way unchecked
With kindness jumping out first
Before the kerfuffle is caused by the chief of social service.

Its casualties remember,
For they are troubled seekers,
Where some reach for the ejection button
Cause the cracked system seeks trouble
Thereby condemning the innocence under the social service.

Only the offspring know
Only they can speak the truth,
Whereby in the absence of kindness
And greed is there to replace it
Only one thing can come to rule the social service...
Negligence!

The Nightwalk of Adolescence

There is a time we all must walk,
Wake up to world holding no stock
To the chimes of an old life left behind
So, I grab a hold of the future that which was assigned.

The future no one imagined possible
Coming out of a family, which it seemed impossible
That anything bright would emerge
Having gone through hell and yet instead I surged

Onward toward the light out of the night,
Seemingly continuous till midway through my plight
In the secondary years of my young life
And internally I knew I would live through my strife.

Wishful Thinking

With many of live wires entwining my delicate mind
With many of cautious creatures obsoleting ever more
Evermore to grasp the wild hand of wishful fancies
For my deepest desires for healing flees me once more
Once more denied the glimmer of solid normality.

Old guides from my old dream wither with the sand,
With the times; as new guides uncover their ugly faces
Their ugliness prevailing through their utopic charade
Quivering into the light of their greedy or perhaps but
Needy need to fill the deepening void of their altercations.

This I knew and a lot more indeed thanks to the old ones,
for they knew a spade was nothing more than a spade
And a liar always lies, and takers always take
and remains forever more the same old same old
never changing with no apologetic tones.

In this I've seen the sparks fly, the flames igniting
Nothing there to still my palpitating heart
And despite the words of rite from the wise
I only think of the errors made and replicated
By the wishful thoughts of the social service…

Because this feeling was replicated from my own family,
My biological family.

Keep on Walking

Here I am just walking the experience,
Just treading the turbulent waters of my life.
Here I am tied to life roulette, willing myself on
No matter how many daggers come flying
That narrowly miss or even the ones that bite.

Time is my strange friend in this strange life,
At once it gives me the sweet illusion
At others, it takes away my free breath,
So live, love, laugh till your dying breath
Cause life is short—the only true words thereby told.

Keep on walking, not dwelling on what's passed
Stand firm toward this future
Cause nothing lasts forever, the good or the bad
And I say all wounds will heal, if only in an allotted time
So, strive forward, don't only survive, but thrive!

Prophecy of a Whim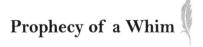

There are some things all which forgot:
A casualty of this age of entitlement.
Only one seems to recall its importance
In an age where security is their newfound lover,
Who impregnated its negligence with undeniable rage.

Although few in number, few do remain
Those who remember those sacred words
That hold healing properties to the broken
Foundations of a lost childhood in the system
That danced with the child's security.

And so, she took the boy on a whim
And cast her spell upon him
Instilling him with encouraging words of kindness
And something weird occurred to the neglected child:
He believed in himself and looked beyond to a bright future.

Only Human

"There is a crack in everything, that's how the light gets in,"
as the late Leonard Cohen would say.

Distractions sprout every year like dandelions,
That once they bloom and turn grey.
A gust blows them astray and gives way
To more guilty pleasures that suck real life
From the real-world experiences beyond.

From birth, we are told to absorb the sage's chant,
Yet those words ring on deaf ears and shan't
Change those who play with the drugs of media
And new age gimmicks to distract us indefinitely
To gloss over the pins and needles of this walk of life.

In this complicated disaster, in this rendition
In this distractaholic era, I survive in between
The manic episodes of this mental matinee
As I watch the players play with my future,
While I'm struggling with the balance of work and play.

Pondering the Parental Reflection

Standing still gazing into the parental mirror,
They tell us like father like son, like mother like daughter
So distinctly I remember when those words were thrown
Like javelins made to pierce flesh and spirit to eternalize
The philosophical meaning of the apple and the tree.

Flames engorge in the beating furnace
Pumping flaring emotion through my veins.
I see it in me, I see it in her
I am skipping and repeating
As the playing needle scraps across my life.

No! No! No! Mustn't there be another way?
I gaze at mother's reflection—reflecting me
I am changing into her as she is becoming me,
Two sides of the same coin, like others had warned,
But the moonlight shadow still casts another outcome.

I inhale, I exhale
Time is walking with me, by my side,
So I shatter the mirror's reflection
And let time do the rest.
I am not my parent's reflection!

Take Hold of Those Wild Reins

Forever remember the ghosts of your past
Let what remains in your past in the past
You are the horse master of your life
Take hold of those wild reins,
And let your past shape your future.

Forever remember who you are,
So take heed and stay strong
For how else would I survive,
So move on, move forward, let go
And take hold of those wild reins
Allowing your past to govern your future.

Forever remember the trauma of your past
Learn as I have from your mistakes
Take that cotton and stow it in your mouth
And not your ears so you can listen
And learn to take hold of those wild reins
To sculpt your past and create your future.

Forever remember yourself, your friends
Don't let yourself fade like wispy ghost,
Let yourself shine within your spirit
That lets you take hold of wild reins
And snap your dark past into your most deserved future.

Ceremonial Farewell to Adolescence

Here I am! I made it
After being a thousand deep
In hormonal, not to mention emotional
Wounds made to test the mentality
Of a thousand deep
In real-world auditions.

Sure, place us all on pedestals
We deserve it, after all
Although we are a thousand deep
In unanswered philosophical questions
Of thousand deep
In financial limbo. (How do we now get through the next
level?)

Yeah, some of us inherit
The cure for financial plague
Hell, some are those deemed gifted
Are a thousand deep
in scholarly gifts given
by whom claimed better luck next year,
and mother whispers in your ear
Why can't you be like him…or her?

And for those who hadn't chose
Their inherited dysfunction
In their parental design.
How are you to deem one worthy?
To deem one undeserving of equal chance,
To see one a thousand deep
In personal tribulations
In financial limbo.

Now I stand high up on the stage,
Ready to receive a piece of paper
And a golden handshake before
I enter the real-world
Naked in my knowledge
To sink or swim depending
On my ability alone
With my instable past
Still lingering in my well-being
With my stress level beaming
Like that annoying cousin
That never shuts up.

"Flash," "flash," "flash" go the memory catchers.
So I stand waving my dark adolescence behind me.

Prattling with My Emotions

Now having been excommunicated out of the system,
I stand on the precipice of the next stressful chapter
On whether I have therefore chosen the correct path.
Happily, they waved goodbye after shaking my hand,
After handing yet another piece of paper meant for atonement.

As if a piece of paper could pay for my books,
my ungodly tuition or even for rent.
Congratulations! You survived! They may as well say too!
And now good luck out there; we're rooting for you!
Our so prized ward who managed not to jump ship.

Sorry did I say that out loud? Sorry, Sally,
I know your mother snorts in her spare time,
And your alcoholic father's in prison again,
But I'm sure this new family is fine—no drugs here!
What do mean about the fresh bruises on your left arm?

Oh, my god, how could this have happened?
Sally's on the news, if only she had a special certificate
To protect her from her mental demons
Or the other families for that matter,
The power of paper compels you!

Sigh, perhaps I was their greatest achievement,
But frankly it didn't leave me unscarred
Being skewered with throbbed emotions,
And it's a bloody miracle that I too hadn't jumped ship,
But as they say stubbornness of goats die hard.

Sure, my fluency in anger was well learned,
And I goddamn earned it, but
The truth of matter is I have come to an understanding,
Despite my confidence being the heaviest casualty,
Despite this old goat still climbing through life.

Have I mentioned I have a few greys?
Surprised, I don't have more! Really, I am!
Hell, at this point, my personal preferences in humans
Is benign to the other sappy jazz going on!
Oh, he's cute … but check out that bosom!

Maybe I am confused, just a bit
Confused as to why we have these choices
And not others, like you can't choose your family
But maybe you can, only you can decide.
Finally, I decided it was all worth it.

Waning Confidence Wanderer

Within the blackest of my shadows,
I wandered through aimlessly,
Thinking I've broken my chains, thus I have left behind
With the last family that once again fell apart.
A numbing coldness sweeps in through my pores.

Seeing only the plumes of exhausted breath,
I breathe in my memories, reexperiencing every misstep
Hopelessly wishing to reexperience my high school years
And relive the experience more collected and level headed
Then I watch the YouTube of my mind, and remind myself:

I still survived, and remained alive
Still as my confidence wanes
After receiving new grades ranging from C–F,
Am I really as bright as they say?
No, it's not that, it's that my talents were elsewhere…
So I continue to wander, for I am the Wanderer.

Breathe the Free Air Again

Go on, take your first free breath, I say
Indeed, each tribulation was another play
Among your strings attached to limbs
Once forgotten to the whims
Of socialistic fantastical flirtations with the SS.

Over the hills, I climbed over doubtfulness,
Nobody shared nor cared to believe
In that all children deserve, every child
Denied the protection from idealistic proclamations
Only meant to earn the popular vote.

For remember now you are free, not quite dumped
On the door step of the depths of your future
Opportune intentions 'cause now I am not weighed down
By the limitations of my social worker
Who only know one language "forget about it."

And despite the mental slashings
Between the cogs of the system I am still breathing, still living
Still able to take a hit for the team,
And I am still able to fight for my bright future.

Tasting Freedom Finally

Let it be, let it go, be free
Give yourself a count of three:
One: your shackles have been unshackled.
Two: feel the weight uplifting from your spirit.
Three: don't forget to breathe deeply.

Oxygenate your soul with kind regards,
Believe me, you're coming around your next boulevard,
Where there'll be more industrial parks,
Waiting to offer you a chance to play the game
Known only as Keep Away: The Adult Version.

I say once more: oxygenate your soul,
So, lose your rigidity; don't fret about your virginity either;
That comes in time, just like when they cut you lose.
I remember how it throbbed with loneliness.
However, allow yourself to taste this freedom.

Spread your wings and take flight
Despite, your past having great plight.
I say this having fought with negative mentalities,
I say this having still made the adolescent jump
And then I realized I'm not even half way there yet…
So, take a breath, you'll need it for the road ahead.

Mother Figure in Need

Crash! Crash! Crash! The brass gongs resonate,
While her intentions decided to reciprocate
The signs of memory hemorrhaging out of her brain,
While pins are stuck into her sciatic backside,
Paving the way to another long road.

She flips, she flops, her veil envelopes
Her cracking sense of right or left or right again,
Becoming that hard and stale cookie that crumbles.
Feeling justified in her age, she lets helping words
Pass through one ear and out the other.

It is now in this time, I remember
Who unlocked that cage long ago,
Back when grain was careless tossed in
And the water jugs poured overhead
Washing over the nervous-noivous mess standing before you.

Her voice was like wind through a windchime,
Emphatically expressing the importance of kindness,
Giving me the taste of well-deserved freedom
And the well-earned love of the beloved family
That was chosen for what my biological one wasn't.

The choice between us was equal,
Despite being after the great fall,
She still remembered the great kindness
Of giving the less fortunate a fighting chance,
And now she is a mother figure in need.

Shedding the Old Cloak

Flip over your black cotton hood,
And I say it has dawned upon the wonder one,
For always I have been known as an anomaly
An anomaly in a system programmed for failure
As it is run by the airhead gallery.

Inhale, exhale your newfound dreams,
As life isn't as bad as it seems.
Storms now passed dissipate ever further away,
As I am still learning to walk and stay
Within my path beyond the shadows of what's passed.

Pull the strings and shed the old cloak,
Now weighing down your talents
Longing to burst free of your self-imposed constrictions
For your spirit must be allowed to grow
Into your new gyrating and capitalizing aura.

Held on only by the frayed cotton seams,
Only as strong as your desire to hold on
To your pass misgivings, so I plea,
"Stop dating with fear because it can't be healthy
And that relationship can only use you...
And leave you dried and emotionally hollow."

Approaching the End of the Tunnel

I keep walking through
All dank and damp, this tunnel, so long and hard
I look forward, not over the shoulder,
Where darkness is all but black pitch
Where the old feelings keep creeping up
As I continue to venture aimlessly forward.

Something is in this musky air,
Causes the happenings and playthroughs
Of this family-related board game, kind of like Jumanji
Except instead of setting loose killer mosquitoes
Or unleashing the entire safari into a stampeding migration,
You see an assault of mental voices, on a mental level spoken
by others.

And yet a bright light twinkles at the opening
At the tunnel, it's coming faster now
Having been long and drawn
In this struggle to move forward
From my experiences, out of this dark cavern.

Healing in Time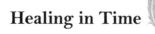

All things in time,
That is what they say
To me, a ward soaked in the slime
Of my biological play.
All things in time—in a time filled with negativity.

Kneeling down by the riverbed,
Having made it through the dread
Of questionable survivability of that time,
When my heart was the subject of Michelangelo
Having been carved by circumstance like his *David*.

Following the river's flow
I found it led to several pools aglow,
Each pool connected to the next
A few had muck clogging the free flow
And not until I cleared the muck did everything flow.

Learning to Walk Again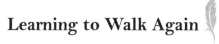

Outgoing ongoing is my shapeshifting personality,
For I am dancing with changing perceptions of myself,
Who am I? Who am I?
For years, people denied my human existence
For years, I have exhibited undying resistance,
Constantly driven to prove my outstanding notoriety.

I lie in a lump on my side—emotionally crippled
Having lost the sublime fruits of expression
Having forgotten the taste of hardy inclusions
Instead being bathed in unforgiving seclusions.
Yet I reach for the hands of the seldom kind.
Those who seem more concerned with themselves.

Now having the necessary hands of support,
I shakily stand, my footing wavering evermore
From the sense of doubt and distrust
I can't trust anyone; how can I trust them?
Yet they remained, still holding my scorned body.
With them … I take my first steps … till I become somebody.

I Am the Throwback Kid

If one could reach in and pluck my soul
Out of my chest one could attest
To the strain of my past sentence
In social welfare and foster care.
Within, one could see the events tattooed on the large blue orb.

They were from a past generation—the good old day
generation
Empathizing with those of the now generation
Getting caught in the dust of financial regression
Created by the confetti generation, who forgot to teach
The Y generation how to socialize and to humanize.

Living with them, being raised by them,
Their sweat from hard work has rubbed onto me,
Causing me to cringe at the signs of desocialization
With the others of my generation wired into their
handheld devices,
Deafening their ear drums, blinding their peripheral sight.

In tonight's news, a teenage girl gets hit by train
Cause: couldn't hear it coming—her earbuds were in,
And yet teenagers of my generation aren't required canes,
Even as the results were clear as rain.
A school now holds their hands praying why and how.

That is not to say, let me please say,
Not all are lost and plugged into the digital matrix,
Some of have learned as I have the ways of the force
Staying in touch with our human necessities
Through the fantasies of twenty-first century entitlements.

No, I didn't have Facebook back then.
Still I barely know what to do with twitter. (It's for twits I
tell ya.)
What's Snapchat for?
No, I'm not going to tell you, what I'm doing on the throne.
I have a life thank you very much.

Old Chains Will Break

Not long ago I sat slump in my chains
Chains that were embedded into flesh of limb and spine
Cauterized by the flames of an unnatural past
With the unnatural paternal influence of an unspoken beast.
Even as these old chains break I will never not feel the pain.

Fear plays the game of fear fueling my own fears
Of losing all that which falls into the crazy category
To be shut up in a hospital room strapped in for the long hall.
Shall I become my own figure of my own fate?
Will I too lose all that I hold most dear—to the sickness of
the mind?

I look up, ignoring the physical and emotional pain
With the chains aching with every motion.
I extend myself to the end of the final twisted link,
And lurching ever forward, the rusted metal whining,
Before finally bursting free, tearing the flesh…

And even as I'm bleeding, I never stopped running
And I never turned back.

Resound and Rejoice

Resound—rebound from the fate of the fading battleground
Wake up and soak in the light of survival
So, I seek out against the bleak till my hidden talents leak
Onto the blank page, bleeding into the flowing words from
the sage
And empower yourself beyond the holy tower who in all
shall cower.

Reality invites me to take a breath and refresh my outlook,
And grasp the hand of renewal and keep striding forward.
I step in to embrace my former self, whom now is left on
the shelf,
And waltz the rigidity out of orientation and discover
its meaning,
And explore the possibilities of unity with
breathtaking continuity.

Ceasing the ever-going pendulum of change cannot hope
for happiness,
For the shrill cry of my outward personality is bursting to
take flight,
Takes a peculiar step into the light without a shred of doubt
Taking heed that any prostrating lout shall not—shall
not interfere
With the resounding rejoice of a thousand gifts only
now provided.

Hierarchical Resistance

So long, auf widersehen, to the voice of past experiences
Long seeking the revolutionary essence within black
sheep tendencies.
Constantly twisting and turning, terminally in revolt
In spite, that I remained in contrite within this social hierarchy.

Wandering within mortal fog that envisions that dreadful flog
Of reality creeping up—catching up within my being
Causing the irreparable blight of foul deeds:
A vexing to me: What must I do for myself to forgive myself?

Though continuing aimlessly through, I resist unwaveringly
Toward those of the ancient generation many years before,
Yet wanting nothing more than some great relief
from the common adolescent belief in their hormonal grief:

Thus, created forever more potent in times of trauma,
Maybe I am making this a nonsensical drama,
But I do know of evil things thronged in the system
Devoid of the common senses that seem to miss them.

So, can anyone blame me for my caution,
My being hollowed of trust—becoming obsequious
Even within this family that which I chose
Whom showed me all what my own could not.

The Waltz through White Smoke

Smoke comes drifting in, caressing my entire being
Even as cloud nine's smile shifts my soul's focus.
Wandering with the mirage of beauties coming hither
To tease my mind's desire to try both flavours.
Before the intoxicating smoke disperses once more.

On the outside, one sees he works hard, is straight-faced,
but muted.
Inside one sees, he dances, is a wild child, and quite observatory.
Inhaling, I choke on the expectation of left or right.
Exhaling, I cough out the realization of the temporal light
Peeking through the veils of my yearning young soul.

I am kissed with the prevailing winds—blowing smoke—
Swirling—waltzing evermore whirling in cyclonic wavelengths
Seen yet not seen between the sublime meetings
Of the two halves waiting to join the game
Everyone else seems to be playing with little belittlement.

I look back, perpetually in reminiscence—remembering
All the instances of a past which scorned my hallowed soul
Having been struck by beast or machine: having remained
Breathing, living, surviving, and somewhat thriving
Recalling evermore of the astounding luck this brave
soul had…

To still be alive, despite having every reason to throw in
the towel.

Spring Off—Of the Offspring

Choked by the ghost of my troubled upbringing
I croak—I revoke the notion of the golden childhood
Soaked in the rivers of time flow awaiting the next chapter
For the origin of this sweet little crow waiting to take flight
And seek the purity within the child now seen impure.

Provoked by the guide of prevalence in our mentality
I awoke—I spoke of the times of martyred kindness
Feeling that honesty became the other casualty
In a world where unfortunate children are cast away
As hopeless cases waiting for hollow pain to end.

Soaked by these rouge waves decisions that overwhelm
So I poke—I stroke at the possibilities of better opportunities
Despite having my past entwined in broken connections
Therefore, creating a record of loneliness and failures,
But looking up I see the next door is just ahead.

Stoked by such thought of renewal in my peace of mind
Hence, I broke—I cloak my adolescence with promise
Where my salvation is in my sense of will in this world
Coupled with my slow forgiveness of my shaky foundation
From which I was raised, but still managed to remain standing.

Strained by the chains of transition I begin to see
And I stray—I pray to hope I remain mentally strong
Through these new experiences built against you
Dominated by the haves who limit the have nots
Who also only provide peanuts instead of free education.

Drained by the ordeals by *care* I revealingly wane,
For the first time, I splay—I spray scorned fire in retribution
Before the dawn of newly formed confidence rises within
Before I begin to learn to walk, head up and not balk
And freeze upon the thought of past strife in the system.

Stained by the flawed will of the woman in green,
Yet I slay—I pay with the strength of stubbornness
That runs in my veins, and maybe I am the only one
Who chose to utilize this sole inheritance and climb higher
Beyond the sentencing of my messed-up background…

So I chose to spring off the baseboard
As the only offspring gifted to do so.

Call of the Wandering Dancer

Everybody stands round and round in perplexity
Recalling the first instance of complex sexuality.
Looking left and right I see my natural conformity
While the murmurs shimmer among this graceful formality,
Waiting for the needle to touch down and make the record sing.

As the bow glides across the strings, our hearts move
To the four-step count: one two three, one two three
As we embrace each other's timid figure, narrowly missing
The feet trying follow the rhythm of the fiddle's waltz
While a warm light fills our pale, spotless visages.

Synchronized in every romantic beat, and I swallow
With the rise of my racing heart, and while quarter turning
she mellows
And with her delicately chiseled features, I begin to sweat
In my growing nervousness, pretending I'm not this
uncoordinated calamity
But she follows, skipping no hip sway, when we start to fly.

Pleasure takes over, our stories fade to the background
Our warmness hand in hand comes to the foreground.
Thinking has left the classroom, as we continue holding
One another, afraid to let go and flop over each other
Taking further advancements to dance to our graceful recovery.

Voice of the Once Forgotten

My mind—deep in heavy sleep
My body—still active letting my mind seep
As I'm wandering these halls late at night
Muttering under my breath in a shaken fright, "Where's James?
Is he okay?"

Suddenly, a hand grasps my own
A whisper echoes through, "He's fine. He's at home."
Gently guided back, I wake; my eyes open wide—
Awakening fully
She told me, "Go back to sleep."

Buzz—buzzzz—buzzzzz tap + swipe—James is dead
Thump, thump, thump-thump, thump
My heart skips a thump, and scars tear
A thought occurs
Did I sense something back then?
Was the delirium just delirium
It had been so long—so long since
He moved to Univer-City
On the mountain with his family.

Regrets now pierce this innocent soul
To what was once an unbreakable bond
Now forever broken with the final caretaker
Having taken his harvest a little premature
Like a tomato gardener who plucks his fruit too soon
Whilst it's still green and inedible.

They say ignorance is bliss
Only now I feel remiss
Once I discovered there was no other
To comfort his invisible wounds
To bandage a heart crevassed in pain.

To the voice once forgotten,
I say I never knew
I ask myself why?
I stand over the wooden box
Saying farewell to my dying past
In my friend's remembrance
In my mental strength, I shall not weigh myself with guilt
Knowing I will remember your existence, and your story.

Breathe In—Breathe Out

Breathe in—breathe out—and breathe deeply
Feel the weight expel itself from your lungs.
Breath in—breathe out—and breathe indefinitely
Through each episode of your personal sitcom
Breathe in—breathe out—and breathe purely.

Find balance in—find balance through—and balance your life
Remember what Michelangelo saw in you
So find balance in—find balance through—and balance despite
all your turmoil
Because Michelangelo saw beauty in your imperfections
Find balance on—find balance through—and balance
yourself true.

Break it—break down—and then break beyond
The strings attached to our emotions
I want you to break it—break it down—and break forward
From your unspoken vow of emotional silence
So break this cycle—break it down—and break loose
From your self-handcuffed shackles
And bare the risk of feeling your feelings.
I know, I had to relearn to feel too.

Pendulum at the Crossroads

For years, I've walked this crooked path
Given the hand of the devil's wraith
Wishing myself back for a do-over
In this life soaked in this clear fluid spillover.
And yet I still approach the pendulum crossroad.

At one end is the penultimate end
At the other is a vision of security
Of friends—of happiness spilled open
From the pain of old wounds caused long ago.
But the pendulum still swings: back and forth.

Chains still cling to the disheveled heart
Aching to pump emotion back into the soul
And return to the brief instance of normal
Felt in between birth and familiar togetherness
And feel the warmth of love and flesh together.

It's still possible
I know it is.

Remember, Bear, Build
(Build Up from Your Origin)

Keep walking from old fates which fades
In a world within a world of emotional raids.
Bear the weight of troubled upbringing
And stand against the need for parental clinging
For the beginning is now, as you live in recovery.

Build from the distinct facades of previous doubts
And armour yourself in your self-pronounced charades
Made only to protect your soul from the real demons
That can drag your world asunder into mental waves
That influx certain emotions into warping distortion.

Saying onto you, as an experienced observer
Advising you to be a mental preserver
To preserve your mental wellness
With those imbued with unbridled kindness
And clear your pools of all the collected muck.

Paths lay before your timid feet
The path behind crumbles into dust
Leaving behind an empty void
Just as you lift one foot in front of the other
You feel a tugging toward the blackness.
But before you let go from the strain
Remember the path is still ahead,
Because you had the strength to remain
Walking continuously forward despite the dread
Clinging to the sight of good future waiting…

For you to let the past go and build up from it
as your solid foundation.

D.M. FERGUSON

Pendulum of the Confused Mind

Chills still ripple through my back
And I cringe as their claws sink deep
With their words of hushed pleas
And please why must you preach
Child protection with your head
Turned 180: possessed with wishful
Thinking feeding me with get-well
Pills only warping my mind
With a hapless tease of normality.

Oh lord, how am I to choose
Right or wrong, left or right, man or woman, happiness
or correctness?
When the fact is, it is all subjective
To the paradigm of the flavor of this generation;
Hoping to change the world's theme
For the better, although some of it works
It doesn't mean it is without its imperfections
Which naturally is in constant reexamination
Of the SS, and yet at same time still allowed to remain,
nearly unchecked.

So please excuse my illicit behaviour, my queerness,
My silent protest
And let's be honest here: all queerness wants
is to say, "Hello, here I am!"
and like desire which was arranged to marry greed
I still receive
Their text messages in my mind's eye
wanting a black and white choice
while reality tells me to smoke them together

to let them rise to the skies
and have the breeze blow it into the past
and try not to attempt to choke
grey smoke with bare palms
or smolder over hot flames
and let them make contact lenses
for your heavily reddened eyes
letting pain stream into the slit
between your tight lips.

And wave at your mental illness
And let it drift in the breeze
even as circumstance calls
for its return trip
but remember what's important...
and uncork your bottle
full of aged expressive wine
and pour a glass of emotion
and sip on happiness.

Don't conform to the dictatorship
of correctness
of the common flavours of *fine*
of a fucked up past
an insecure infrastructure
a neurotic disturbed shell
a post traumatic emotion disorder
and remember
to talk to that old friend...happiness
who only wants to take your hand
and embrace you.

D.M. FERGUSON

Learning to See beyond the Black and White

Today is my reckoning day
or maybe it's not
maybe it'll be tomorrow
or the next day or the day after that—
in that I reckon times are changing.
My times, your times, our times
all from good to bad—bad to good.

The fog rolls in.

We must keep walking
clinging less relying less
on the white cane
of false confidence
tapping the borders of personality.

Speak your truth!
Speak your anxiety!
Speak your depression!
Speak your fears!
Speak your language!

The language of your past
even with the bombardments
of "can't" and "no"
which drain and bellow

Teach yourself to walk
Without the shackles of past experiences.

I know it's tough to bear
such weight.
I know it's rough to go
in between those grinding systematic gears.

Yet nothing is immortal
Pain can fade.

Just say "goodbye" and forbade
its return
and release it
and let it fly into nothingness.

Guide yourself through the fog.
Write it down in your personal blog
and let happiness pierce through your retinas
like a laser eye surgeon
trying to restore your distorted vision
and allow your sight to return
and clear the fog created by the black and white mind
and make your future vision
of the self
a brighter
reality.

Mental Spring Cleaning

Take a seat.
Close your eyes.
Breathe deeply.
Exhale
and gaze at your inner self.

Sit alone.
Imagine white light.
Let it enter you.
Pleasure you.
Comfort you.
Caress you.

I come standing on insight
only here after such plight
wanting to take flight
from this endearing new sight.

The red door opens with retorts
And I am greeted with emotion
Hello, happiness!
Hello, reality,
where have you been after all this time?
I walk through
to an open and lush valley
and in the deepest part
a serpentine stream
winds down toward the rolling hills below.

It flows out of sight
into the misty woods.

A long series of stone steps snaked
down into the heart of those misty woods.

A step taken
and a breath breathed
and I stepped further down those steps
my mind shifting
as I am making my way
into those woods.

And I close my eyes
before opening them again
where I am then transported
inside deep in the woods.

The stream flowed closely by,
flowing freely
in and out
of seven swirling pools.
Till I gaze closely
at the fourth and seventh pools
where muck, moss, and old man's beard
clogged the outflow of cool water.

Going closer I grab a slender stick
and poke timidly at the clogged outflow
lifting the locked free flow of the stream
and allow the stream flow faster and more naturally.

I take the stick and do the same
for the seventh pool of swirling clean water
clogged with muck.

Standing there contemplating
these swirling pools of pure water.
I begin to feel at one with myself…

And I close my eyes to open them
in the here and now.

Breathe in
Breathe out
Clear the muck
and let the stream flow freely
in your life
having lived through your grief.

Facing the Flames Which Burned

The memory remains imprinted
on my brain
burned by its chameleonic personality,
shifting to match the voices from nowhere.

No! I want it now!
Stay away from Burnaby, it's too expensive!
Get out! Get out! Get out!

These words echoed
his actions showed
the instability
of his ability.

And now the flames which burned
are presently in baggage claim
looking much like others
some darker, some lighter
and after a while someone
comes along to claim it.

One, who carries the same baggage
Share the same stories,
the same flames,
the same scars.

Just learning the language of reprieve.

I wondered what my past meant,
only now I guess I repent,
that I will discover it,
as my future sprints
and my past stumbles behind,
only now I begin to know…
how to bear the flames which burned.

Let It Flow

Survived?
Good, breathe in and out
and congratulate with all who went in ordeal.

Swim in between the lines of the system
and forgive the lies that seep through the cracks.

There are many who walk the same path,
and don't even make it three steps in,
but you survived the walk.

Take out the pins from your own voodoo doll,
instead of letting sink ever deeper into flesh.

Much muskeg has collected over time,
but much of this sorrow is not worth my dime,
when it clogs, and weighs down my natural self.

Let it flow down the river into the past.
Since you're a survivor, you will always last.

D.M. FERGUSON

Flirting with My Duality

Having wandered a long, long time
on many a turbulent path,
I thought of it as an afterthought.

There comes a time when adolescence
flips the coin of gender,
and with whatever side it lands
is the calling the soul.

In all the comings and goings,
I noticed the new flavours
drifting past,
drawing my wandering eye.

For me, the coin landed vertically,
leaning against a chair leg,
and yes, I like people like I do my food
with a little bit of everything.
I find both flavours intriguing
both having their highlights and lowlights.
Neither are the perfect choice
even if it isn't a choice.

Holding the Trigger

Looming over the cliff's edge,
the silver barrel kisses my temple.

Never seen by the naked eye, but it leaves a wedge
in the heart of my crumbling and sacred temple.

Pulling the trigger—I blow out nullified emotion
letting the weirdness like blood
flow out and seep through the pores
of my insecurity like flesh

and in a single motion
I leap out
and glide among the night's stars.

Then the memories flashback,
that do all but bring back
the lengthy journey, I have walked
the kind we all walk.

And I wonder about my bounce back
then again maybe I am holding the trigger—
the trigger to my success, and maybe I'm holding myself back.
The silver barrel is lifted away.

Earthbound Roots
(Remembering Your Origin)

Beaten and battered down the old path.
Shaken, twisted, and torn by cold ideals:

Let it lie, dust to dust,
ashes to ashes
and let it strengthen your aura.

Flash! Snap! Snap-snap!

II

I am here, sucked dry of comfort,
standing timidly before the observers
of my long walk to freedom—now observed.

First beginning with family
soaked in melancholy, poisoned with
spent pleasing efforts of love.

III

Together, we are connected
through string theory,
where our world's follow
similar paths with various outcomes.

I am here, still alive, still to persevere
and depart with my sullen heart.

It was the great struggle,
wishing myself to be a non-muggle,
having fallen to the bottom of the barrel,
drowning in the success of others.

But remove yourself with the concern of others,
look at yourself still alive, despite such respite
in your crooked journey through the game of life.

Bathe in your undiscovered talents
return to your remission
and let the cancerous memory fade
with happiness and freedom of being yourself
being allowed to flow in with your shackles falling to clatter
on the ground with your broken soul.

Era of the Withered Ward

Time is that fickle friend,
changing in favour of the end
of the one who gathers no will.

Emotions may now lie in tethers,
But know you've survived all weathers
staying grounded with the ones who have it.

Life will only become a broken record,
if you forget your true accord
with your true self in your given time.

So lay down this era of the withered ward
And let rest your swelled emotion hoard,
and release the chains of your shaken will.

It's your life
now live it.

The Iron-Grey Wolf

Making it to the edge while pondering the experience, long
and hard
Over the course of abandonment and neglect,
while I recalled, nearly weeping, suddenly summoning
every honourable memory of the Iron-Grey Wolf.

Forever she had led the broken—
only now she is the one broken—
never to recover, despite always fighting.

Shuttering, I recall the first time I met you—
you, who inspired me to be me
and with each dying breath pulls at my heartstrings,
while you lay collapsed—exhausted from your cancerous fight.

I remain committed to the might
of your words to tell me to face my plight.

And of the sad reminiscence of every ill-fated hunt
for a stable home environment
killed me—instilled in me with doubts never
felt on such a level before;
so I loom over her—gazing into her exhausted eyes, thinking,
"Will I ever be able to see myself soar?
As you lay dying, knowing you will never see me soar—
this is goodbye, my beloved mentor."

Just as your final breath escapes your lungs,
I utter, "thank you for the experiences,
thank you for being what my father couldn't,
thank you, for giving me a chance in this hardened life."

As my soul grows stronger, I will shy away no longer,
as forever you will never be forgot
as forever you will remain a piece of my heart
as forever I will remember you gave me a shot
and now it's your turn to rest, and I promise I will never
fall apart.

Part Two:
Other Memories of the Crows

Breeze in the Setting Sun

Looking upward toward the sky,
letting the cool breeze relieve my wet eye,
feeling the colours of the concluding day,
which shine, while the winds whistle through the pine.

The iron-grey wolf rests.

Now the young pup can attest
to the memories well spent
though too quickly they went,
but still are carried on in the memory
of the iron-grey wolf.

Darting forward,
I pump my legs evermore,
recalling her, as the crumpled brown leaves are blown
and drift with the gentle breeze
only to kiss the sea of memories,
in which they may decay over time,
but its beauty will vividly remain
in my mind
just like the good times through this arduous journey.

Synthesis within the Pines and Oaks

Out from the past,
I run in between the vast
succession of the winds
following the energies for calming minds
within the shades underneath the canapes.

In the lightness within the air
of the lush greens, I gleam
as the warm sunlight kisses
the nape of neck, but misses
my naked pupil, so not so blinding.

A gust billows.

The pines sway listlessly,
while the oaks creak and bellow:
the branches release their grenade like cones
exploding with beauty with the sunbeams
as their spotlight.

Around the next bend,
I find the largest oak tree
Toward which I trot,
the roots' base vacant
of where I will plop
myself down
and close my eyes
and ears to the city buzz
to breathe in wet air
and exhale negative polluted air.

To observe the birds flying
over passed
the bees buzzing by
the skeeters singing too high
within sensitive eardrums.

And in doing so, I expel
from my lungs
from my pores
from my aura
in a single breath
all insecurities
all anxieties
overall negativity
from my delicate being
with my patience, all but spent.

Then I inhale
potential prosperity
potential recovery
a potentially bright future
no one else ever imagined.

Inhale—exhale
Inhale—exhale
Inhale—exhale

Through my closed eyelids
the sunbeams leak through
warming my sight—warming my spirit
chilled since birth.

Falling back on my skill
on my talents of survival,
I challenge the game of norms
of family tradition,
where it had previously failed.

In the sunlight, the past fades.

The path lies ahead.

So I open my eyes
Having absorbed the grounded energy
having temporarily lifted the weight
of a past long since passed,
one that will fade
and become distant memory.

D.M. FERGUSON

Polar Bear in the Glintz

Shimmering in the mirrorlike reflection,
memories flit back to the old days—

while all us shivering campers wait
to take the morning polar bear
dip in the old Glintz Lake.

Mist dances on our flesh
And on the otherwise still water.

We leap in
so our stress seeps out
to be dispersed among the lily pads.

We clamour up onto the dock
and mock the ones who weren't
brave enough,
just as the survivors
stumble
for their towels.
Some
even hopped in the sauna.

Dog Walking along the Dykes

Away from the city,
away from the commotion,
we drive along the winding road
far from the stress left behind.

Lacey sits excitedly,
nose poked out the open window
standing right on the switch
her hind right in my crotch.

Sprinkles of raindrops splatter inward,
while I embrace her runt of a boxer frame,
her stubby tail swinging rapidly,
back and forth.

I slip the leash on her collar.

The silver bridge—we are here.

Hark! Gulls and crows fly overhead.
I open the door.

The kind one right behind me,
and together, we tread the trail
along the Alouette River
with Lacey pulling me along.

D.M. FERGUSON

Biking for Solitude

Off I go,
riding my bike
retreating for much needed recovery.

Birds sing cheerily,
pronouncing the beauty of the warm blue sky.

The gravel grinds under the treads of rubber,
as my wind-brushed face
is torn by troubling things.

I need this escape!

There are spaces
in places hidden
from public viewings.

Around the next bend,
a rushing shadow catches my eye.

It leaps out from the bush.
Squeezing the handle bars,
My gears sing
as I come full stop.

It was a silver-grey coyote,
and its small frame also came full stop
to participate in a sort of staring contest.

We continue staring,
Before it chooses to move on.

My being, bewildered by the encounter,
feeling that there was mental exchange of sorts—an
unspoken message
exchanged between us before moving on.

This day is beautiful.
Move on!
Move on!
Move on!

Let your doubts be gift wrapped
for the evergreens as nutrients,
recall ever so more, that they do
take in our air-like waste
in CO_2
in exchange for their air-like waste
in O_2.

Not far off
is the runoff path,
leading down to the tree above the riverbank
with the view of bridges and sunsets.

Even as steep as it was going down,
I take the risk—risking my own personal injury.

Making it safely down,
I kick the kickstand.

Reaching the tree, I slip off my bag
and plop myself down at the base of its roots.

Breathing in—
breathing out, absorbing the calm demeanour
of a boy
seeking solitude from the city buzz—
buzzing in his mind's eye
from his family pollution of uncertainty.

I unzip my bag
and from my bag
I reach in and pull out
my copy of *Angels & Demons.*

Opening it,
I leave the present world
and transport to the secondary world
within the dry and inked pages
of written imagination,
which enters my own expansive imaginary mind.

As of yet, a man is branded earth,
while the church scrambles for leadership
and the chosen ones are held prisoner,
and the only hope is some guy from Harvard.

The novel changes pages.
Looking up—my gaze interrupted
by beautiful scene drifting by
overhead and across the horizon.

Breathing in—
breathing out, I return to the inner workings
of Dan Brown's plot with the famous symbologist.

Hours pass by like the drifting clouds
and within the pages someone is to be found…*dead,*
deep in a demon's hole beneath a historic church—
now discovered to have been branded with *earth*
with its dirt compacted in the back of his windpipe.

The imaginary image daunting—so daunting.

I close it
save it
like a computer document
saved for the next reading.

I stand,
I wander, over to the edge
of the riverbank
full of stones and boulders.

Upon one of these boulders, I sit—
I contemplate my situation
and think about my incredible luckiness

to be alive
and to still survive
despite the troubled times.

I've escaped that home
in the heart of social welfare
in the city filled with broken dreams and dreamers.

Being aloud to stay in the safe house
on the other side of gloom,
where encouraging bright energy resides
in the heart of social well-being
in the town filled with natural healing energies and healers.

Now to let myself,
it has only begun.

Now to go home,
to have my well-deserved meal,
that until now was not a sure deal.

So I pack my things,
having cleared for the time being,
my mind, body, and soul,
and I mount my bike
and I ride off into the distance.

Island Hopping

Creeping up and over
the golden orb rises over
the mountainous peaks
warming the cold and bleak
backdrop of the day before.

Winds of late mellow
And the waves remain shallow
quiet and gentle
barely lapping at the air
or slapping at our hulls.

Over the hand-pumped stoves,
the oatmeal boils,
other campers stir and bustle
packing up and preparing themselves,
while the councillors stir the pot
tossing in raisins and cinnamon.

Gathering around
in the holy made circle of sacred replenishment,
the nine campers await
with their empty bowls
waiting for warm oatmeal
for the road ahead
instead, the road is ocean.

The sun rises higher
ever gleaming evermore
revealing the perfect beauty
for a day of paddling.

Having consumed everything—
Including every grain,
we pack and stuff
the rest of our things into the compartments
in our plastic kayaks.

All of us slip on our fitted dresses,
and once seated
one by one pulling the straps
over the lips of the cockpit
fitting us in securely
we launch ourselves
pushing ourselves
out toward open sea.

Singly, we align
announcing ourselves a leader,
we follow with our paddles
dipping generously in the saltwater,
moving it in J-like motion
moving the swirling currents
behind us
around us
in between us
and we paddle on,
onward to the next—
to the next gulf island—
to the next rest stop
to the next open beach
to replenish upon.

I glance over starboard,
I notice a bloom of white jellyfish,
drifting passed
six feet below the current.

Stroke. Stroke. Stroke.

Rest.

I slip my hand
Into the cool saltwater
letting relief flow
into my pores
and allow the stress to leak out,
letting my mind enter peace
for the time being.

Memorable Mainland Winter

Silence falls like a showman's curtain.
Winds whistle with the season's change
with the unusual chills, it made this winter uncertain.

Grey clouds gather
the mercury stands in limbo,
fighting to balance the scale
that is between warm and cold temperatures.

The two airs dance
in the snowy waltz.

Each flake now clinging loosely
to fluffy cloud,
before letting go
to gently drift to the earth below.

Soon it flurries,
soon the temperature drops
icicles form like fingernails from the eaves,
but at least school was out for the Christmas season.

Soon the white stuff blankets the lawns, streets, and trees,
while children gather around the windows
with no whine in their voices: they were in awe.
The adults gathered too to peer out the windows
for fear of the inevitable driving conditions
to follow in this uncommon mainland winter.

Black ice forms
Courtesy of Jack Frost,
hoping to ensnare the unprepared in his slippery traps.

People bundled tight as drums,
Puffed up like walking cushions.
This year will be wicked (it's 2008).

***

More and more the flakes fell
having been caught under this chilling spell,
where the snow continued to accumulate
and place onto the hedges with such great weight.

Even the strong oak trees began to feel its strain,
the branches crack.
The sparkling lights upon the little firs drain,
fading beneath the snow.

Even the little three feet tall deer
couldn't be seen
with its warm lights, all one could see.
Inside the firewood cracks
with the radiating warmth filling the living room.
I lounge in the chaise lounge
with my book reading with the snow as my backdrop
outside with the winter's chill
howling against the panes of glass.

The cat leaps up upon the arm,
nestling herself next to me.
The dog nuzzling her nose
against my thigh
then pressing liver lips
upon the protected leather chaise lounge
with her big eyes
casting a spell over my being.

"Awe, very cute Lacey."

And I scratch behind her big floppy ears.

The evergreen tree
heavily decorated
with a beautiful plastic angel
gives off cozy light.

Warmth remains with us
All is good.

Mountainous Driving
(Approaching Halfway)

With the turn of a key, it grumbles,
and with a puff of smoke, it rumbles
and with another click, it shifts into gear
and the silver bullet car drives off with no fear.

Sun kissed with the lips of this wave,
the heat makes the passengers cave
and crack open the window to permit
a cool breeze to cool us a little bit.

Indeed, AC was present,
but this old gent
claimed it burdened his wallet
but to me I call it
Cheapskate or Miser
as in my grandfather.

Just as we approach the Coquihalla
something claws at my stomach,
something stirred—something churned—
Something turned making it do backflips.

Was it the motion of the car?
Or perhaps it was something I ate,
as something inside had disturbed my being.

Maybe it was that banana I had,
Cause I forgot that it affects me on long trips.
Why? No idea.
I shouldn't have had it.

So I lay on my side,
as my eyes black out
with the motion sickness encapsulating me.

I close my eyes,
before I realize
we have arrived
at the Home Restaurant
in Merritt
just approaching the halfway mark.

Mountainous Driving
(Okanagan Abound)

Key inserted
One quarter turn
Putt. Putt. Grumble. Rumble.
The silver bullet comes to life
roaring to go forth.

Gear is shifted,
mirrors adjusted
and grandad steps on the gas
and makes his way out of the lot
and makes the turn toward the Okanagan.

Face now pressed against the window,
I see a movie reel
of beauty
of evergreens
of bright-blue sky
of majestic mountains
with a couple of bald eagles
swooping by
chasing a flock of crow
who were apparently bugging them,
as they didn't appear to be hunting.

Snaking around the bends
the scars begin to unveil themselves
the scars from previous years
from fires
from potential over harvests.

The drybrush underneath
Drier—drier than ever recorded
according to the man in the radio
as grandad was listening to it closely.

Slowly, we approach
the toll booth
to pay the toll of the Coquihalla
and pass on
to the other side.

Other cars pass through single file
one by one
through the gate of our lane.

Some cash is exchanged
Between the gatekeeper
and the great miser
and we all pass on
to the other side
moving merrily through
to the Okanagan Valley.

Road to Cracked Skies

A week it's been
since we've seen
the beautiful mountain scenes
of British Columbia,
having now just entered Manitoba.

Pitch-black clouds gather
and even after
we make it to the next Timmy's
we see the clouds becoming darker
and we hoped it were drifting further
in the opposite direction,
but it was after all
just wishful thinking.

To myself I thought,
Why do I have this feeling?
It's going our direction
isn't it.

Crackle! Crackle! *Boom!*
Deep in the thunderstorm,
there was no turning back.
As lightning touched down
Like fingers of god reaching
to feel the soft soil of earth
in the many farmlands
outside Brandon
inside the third Prairie province.

Even still we take a tour
in a small forgettable old town
a town of one of my foster mum's,
but the clouds not only remained
blacker still,
but also, remained hovering over us,
so we break for highway 1
once more.

Rumble! Rumble! *Boom!*

Another bolt touches down
in the distance.

Then something else occurred.
The clouds seemed to be funneling
making fingers of their own,
wishing to touch earth.

She floors it,
that is the driver,
whom of which
was the better driver.
Luck for us.

Boom!

Yet another strike
the distance, but closer
than the times before.

Funnel clouds remain in the sky.

Hearts were thumping
with the vibrations felt
with last strike.

The driver floors it again,
till finally we approach the Best Western.

Skies flash with warning

Quickly we grab our suitcases
and check into our hotel room.

Ferry to Camp Amusement Park

Racing on
Racing through
the heavy traffic came into view
with the other travelers awaiting
the next ferry to board
toward the capital
on the island.

For the first time
I smell the ocean scent
flowing in through the open window.

Such a refreshing smell it was.

It was the furthest I've been
from my home like prison.

I was so lucky,
having the luck of a fostered ward,
having been forgotten by ones
who should've cared,
but now is not the time
to think about their crimes,
but to chime in
to new experiences
only now being offered.

Other boys and gals gather by
and offered up their luggage.

I do the same.

Then waving goodbye
My foster parents to be
leave me
to walk on with the others
who are bound for Camp Amusement Park
oh sorry, excuse me: Camp Qwanoes.

Ushers usher
the herds of children
into the ship.

I myself am thrilled
I am free
for two weeks.

Immediately I run
for the top deck,
Immediately the horn
drones with deafening power.
My heart skips, startled.

The cool ocean wind
brushes my visage
and massages my sinuses
clears them.

Man, I can breathe out here!

As I recalled the cigarette scent
saturated in the carpets
and walls
and the overall atmosphere
of the prison home left, behind.
Too soon
the ferry slows
before docking
on the other side.

Time moves fast.

Once again
our ushers usher us
off the boat
and onto the line of buses
waiting outside to take us.

Everyone was excited,
like puppies waiting to go for a walk.

Everyone eager to get off
and set foot on Camp Amusement Park (I mean Qwanoes).

After a long drive
we finally arrive,
and everyone cheers
and those who could peers
out to see a tunnel of hands
being set up in front of the doors
of each bus.

The doors open
and all the children run out
spilling into an open field.

Running with His Dog

Bursting out of her master's car door
our pup that we all adore
runs freely in with the breeze,
till I race after her with ease
because she always targets me
when she bolts for me gleefully.

Slipping away into the tall grass,
I lie down and let her pass
around me before returning to me
with her tongue lapping at me,
before I grasp her collar and backside
and hold her till the leash was supplied
by my foster mum not far behind.

Once leashed
our little boxer jumped playfully
blatantly playing tug of war
biting and tugging at her leash.
Even letting her have it,
She insists we have it,
to play with her again.

Till at least a bee buzzes by,
and her jaw snaps—snaps at the buzzing bee
interrupting her gleeful walk.

Witnessing Smoke through Trees

Witnessing of late the smoke that rises
in the outskirts of the valley which surprises
with record-breaking heat, sparking forest fires
and though we are in safe area, one imagines the pyres
of those homes unfortunately caught in this horrible wave.

Wafts of hazy smoke blow through the city,
making breathing around here shitty,
especially one with such breathing difficulty
such as I—even an air-quality warning is issued,
and before long worry swept over and continued
despite my grandparents telling me we'll be safe.

Soon enough, however, I was to be sent home,
knowing full well it will be far better for my lungs.
So I'm informed I am going by Greyhound
and once I am packed I will be homebound
heading back south toward the Lower Mainland,
where the air will be clearer for my asthma.

Here I am at the terminal,
and before I leave my grandad
gifts me with some cash
before saying goodbye.

Clearing the Buzz

Slipping over the bridge like Terabithia
away into a wondrously lush land to recharge
energy once lost to mental buzz of unstable home
caused by the ever-changing nature of the kind one.

Dismounting around the bend, I leave my bike
where I wander off for a little hike.
Then a wisp of cool breeze comes down
and enters my minds clearing any jazz.

I kick off my flip-flops,
pressing the soft pads of my feet
into the earth, allowing the critters
to tap their legs in and out of my toes.

Looking around, I notice cotton balls
drifting in the breeze, as I escape reality.
I slide one hand onto the nearest evergreen,
making it sticky and hot as I glide it
over the moss and sap oozing from the bark.

D.M. FERGUSON

Being the Leaf in the Wind

Holding on to dear things.
Known only to fear things.

Grasping at frail connections
never meant to stay attached
to the central branches of the family tree.

With nothing more than gentle breeze
the coloured leaves break away—drifting ever further
from a well-rooted family tree.

Leaves cannot control the wind
that blows them astray
to gyrate their fragile worlds,
but leaves don't give up
they don't resist
they don't hang
on to old pains.

Leaves blow with the wind.
So we must become a leaf in the wind.

CPSIA information can be obtained
at www.ICGtesting.com
Printed in the USA
BVHW041722241022
650027BV00001B/61